SIMPLY
ADVENT

SIMPLY ADVENT

A JOURNEY OF HOPE, PEACE, JOY, AND LOVE

LISA FAHEY

Farmhouse Publishings

Farmhouse Publishings, LLC
P.O. Box 333
Spearfish, SD 57783

Although the author and publisher have tried to ensure that the information and advice in this book were correct and accurate at press time, the author and publisher do not assume and disclaim any liability to any party for any loss, damage, or disruption caused by acting upon the information in this book or by errors or omissions, whether such errors or omissions result from negligence, accident, or any other cause.

ISBN (Softcover): 979-8-9936057-3-9
ISBN (Ebook): 979-8-9936057-4-6

Design by Heidi Caperton (pineconebooks.com)

Printed in the United States of America.

To our dearest daughters, Alisha and Rebecca,

When I think of Christmas, I think of you. For so many years, I wanted everything to be "just right" and to create the perfect Christmas for you. But one day I realized it was already perfect—because of Jesus, and spending Christmas with you. God ordained that we would share these moments together, and that was more than enough.

My prayer for you is that you will slow down, breathe in the beauty of the season, and truly enjoy the time of preparation before Christmas—Advent. Keep your eyes fixed on the Lord, and you will find that everything is already perfect in Him.

With all my love,

Mom

TABLE OF CONTENTS

WEEK ONE: HOPE

WEEK TWO: PEACE

WEEK THREE: JOY

WEEK FOUR: LOVE

Welcome,

Advent is my most anticipated time of year. As the days grow darker and the evenings arrive sooner, I find myself wanting to slow down and soak in the stillness. While I love the joy of Christmas, my heart is especially drawn to these weeks of Advent—weeks where I can pause and remember all that God has done for us. From the humility of coming as a baby to being born in a stable and lying in a feeding trough, the story of Jesus' birth is full of details that are easy to miss if we rush through the season.

To me, Advent feels like an invitation. It's a time to wait, to watch, and to prepare my heart for Christ. When I light the candles of Hope, Peace, Joy, and Love, I'm reminded that each small flame pushes back the darkness—just as Jesus, the Light of the World, pushes back the shadows in our lives. Advent is more than simply anticipating the arrival of Christmas; it's about observing the divine activities unfolding in the midst of my ordinary routines.

I don't want this season to be filled only with decorating, shopping, or planning. I want it to be filled with presence—with being still, being open, and letting God meet me in the quiet. When I sit with Scripture, whisper a short prayer, or simply pause to breathe, I find that the Spirit makes room in my heart for Christ in ways that surprise me.

My prayer is that as you walk through this season, you too will feel a more profound awareness of Emmanuel—God with us—not just on Christmas Day, but in every ordinary moment of life.

Welcome to *Simply Advent*. Let's step into this season together, slowing down and opening our hearts to the One who has come, who is with us now, and who is coming again.

Lisa

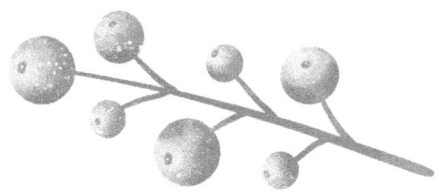

HOW TO USE THIS
ADVENT DEVOTIONAL

Advent is a sacred time of anticipation, tranquility, and preparation. It encourages us to momentarily retreat from the hectic pace of life and open our hearts to Christ—not just in honor of His birth at Christmas, but also for His return. This devotional aims to facilitate daily pauses for reflection, allowing you to welcome Jesus into your life each day. Feel free to engage with it individually, with loved ones, or in a small group setting.

Each day consists of:

- Reflection – A concise devotional to assist you in your prayer and meditation.
- Daily Scripture – A verse to inspire your contemplation.
- Prayer – A heartfelt invitation to engage with the Divine.
- Journal Prompt – A question designed to enhance your contemplation.
- Supplementary Scriptures – Verses for deeper reflection.

Take your time with each section. Read at a measured pace, allowing yourself to reflect, pray, and write in your journal—or simply sit in peaceful silence, attuning your heart to hear God's voice.

On the weekends, you can expect to find:

- A cohesive contemplation on the themes of Hope, Peace, Joy, and Love.
- Instructions for Lighting Candles on the Advent Wreath.

- Questions for reflection to guide journaling or group discussions.
- Extra Scriptures for further study and sharing.

If you are engaging in this as a family, encourage everyone to take part in the lighting of candles, reading Scripture, or leading prayers together. If you are doing this alone, keep in mind that you are joining countless believers who are also preparing their hearts during this sacred season.

If you happen to miss a day, don't worry—just resume from where you stopped. Advent isn't about achieving perfection; it's about making space in your heart for Christ.

Make this devotional a part of your daily routine in a way that suits you best. Whether you enjoy it with your morning coffee, during a lunch break, or as part of your nighttime wind-down, may each reflection bring you closer to God. Allow Advent to softly transform your daily rhythm through the gifts of hope, peace, joy, and love.

I've added a QR code that directs you to a Simply Advent playlist on Spotify—let the music enhance your prayer and reflection. Additionally, there's a QR code for the Leader's Guide, designed to assist small groups and leaders in facilitating discussions during Advent.

LISA FAHEY MINISTRY
SIMPLY ADVENT LEADER'S GUIDE

SCAN ME!

@LISAFAHEYMINISTRY / WWW.LISAFAHEY.COM

LISA FAHEY MINISTRY
SIMPLY ADVENT PLAYLIST

SCAN ME!

@LISAFAHEYMINISTRY / WWW.LISAFAHEY.COM

PREPARING OUR HEARTS FOR CHRIST: THE JOY OF ADVENT

As the world rushes toward Christmas with shopping, decorating, and celebrations, the Church invites us to take a different approach. Advent calls us to pause, take a deep breath, and make room in our hearts for Jesus, in contrast to the secular demands that crowd our schedules and drain our finances.

During Advent, we prepare for the coming of the Messiah. It is not just about waiting for December 25; it is about preparing our hearts to accept Christ every day. This serves as a reminder that our Lord and Savior has come, is with us right now, and will come again at some point. Remembering the past, recognizing the present, and looking ahead provides us with perspective, keeps us grounded in the chaos, and gives us a constant sense of hope.

Advent is beautiful because of what it is. One of the most cherished traditions in the Church is the lighting of the Advent wreath. Each candle—Hope, Peace, Joy, and Love—marks our journey toward the coming of Christ, pushing back the darkness one week at a time. The circle of evergreen branches reminds us of God's eternal love, unending and ever faithful. With every flame that flickers to life, we proclaim that the Light of the World has come and will come again. Reflecting on God's promises, remembering the prophets' longing for the Messiah, and rekindling our desire for His presence are all part of the beauty of this season.

The truth is that being too busy can take away the happiness we're trying so hard to create. When we strive for perfection in everything we do, from presents to meals to traditions, we risk missing the One who loves us even when we are at our messiest. It was in a lowly manger that Jesus came to earth, not in a majestic palace. Subtle and ordinary as it was, His birth was profoundly holy. The season of Advent calls us back to that same holy simplicity.

We are reminded during Advent that rest is sacred. We make room for Christ to live in us when we pause to pray, light a candle, or sit with Scripture. We begin to grasp the profound significance of seemingly little things—being quiet, being kind, simply being still—in preparing our hearts for the greatest gifts.

What is the significance of Advent for us?

Advent shifts our perspective. It gently pulls our focus away from the distractions of the world and draws our hearts back to God. It reminds us to place our longing for Christ above everything else and to make Him our first priority. Not only does Advent lead us up to Christmas Day, but it also makes us ready to welcome Jesus into our lives every day—through prayer, through Scripture, and through the people He places in our path.

During this season, may we prioritize rest over hurry, contemplation over distraction, and Christ above material possessions. This Advent, may we accept God's gracious invitation to quiet the chaos of this world and rest in the peaceful beauty of His presence. In that peace, we recognize the fulfillment of our deepest desires: the presence of God among us, Emmanuel.

WEEK ONE

HOPE

WEEKEND REFLECTION
HOPE

THE PROMISE OF THE MESSIAH

L et us begin this Advent season with hearts open to the great promise that God has given us—the promise of a Savior. Long before Jesus' birth, the prophet Isaiah spoke of a child who would come as a sign of God's faithfulness:

> *Therefore the Lord himself will give you a sign: The virgin will conceive and give birth to a son, and will call him Immanuel. He will be eating curds and honey when he knows enough to reject the wrong and choose the right* (Isaiah 7:14-15 NIV).

Isaiah also proclaimed the hope of a righteous King from the line of David who would bring peace and justice to the earth:

> *A shoot will come up from the stump of Jesse; from his roots a branch will bear fruit. The Spirit of the Lord will rest on him—the Spirit of wisdom and of understanding, the Spirit of counsel and of might, the Spirit of the knowledge and fear of the Lord... The wolf will live with the lamb, the leopard will lie down with the goat, the calf and the lion and the yearling together; and a little child will lead them* (Isaiah 11:1-10 NIV).

A PROPHECY IN A TIME OF CHAOS

There is a powerful narrative in the prediction that reveals the hopes and fears of a society that is about to change. In the eighth century BC, King Ahaz of Judah was about to face a crisis: the armies of Syria and Israel were about to attack his country. In this time of fear and confusion, the prophet Isaiah sent a strong and reassuring message: the miraculous birth of a child named Immanuel.

The significance of this profound statement is that it was a sign of hope and the presence of God. It also indicated that God would always be there for His people, even if things got difficult. People were instructed in the prophecy to be open to change, growth, and development, just like they are now. It enabled people to be more resilient, more creative, and it led to greater happiness that results from trusting God.

The miraculous birth of the Virgin Mary calls our attention to the beauty, grace, and transforming power of faith at the intersection of this world and eternity. In moments of difficulty and doubt, we can seek solace and assurance in the name Immanuel, which means "God is with us." Embracing this truth inspires faith, unity, and a deeper connection with the divine.

A LIGHT IN THE DARKNESS

How does one hold on to hope when surrounded by darkness? It is extremely difficult. Yet when we look to the Lord, He offers us a hope that something better is to come. The opposite of hope is hopelessness—heavy and immobilizing. Prayer, community, and remembering God's promises pull us from that place. Advent is God's invitation to exchange hopelessness for His hope.

This same promise is for us today. When life feels broken, when our world feels heavy, when circumstances press in—we can cling to Immanuel. The Messiah came not only to redeem, but to dwell with us, to carry us through our struggles, and to bring ultimate peace.

PRAYER

Lord, as I begin this Advent journey, remind me that You are faithful to Your promises. Help me to see the light of Christ even when I feel surrounded by darkness. Plant hope deep within my heart and prepare me to celebrate the coming of my Savior with joy, trust, and anticipation. Amen.

QUESTIONS FOR REFLECTION

1. Where do you need to see God's promise of hope fulfilled in your own life right now?

2. How can you prepare your heart to welcome the Messiah afresh this Advent season?

3. What does it mean to you personally that Jesus is *Immanuel—God with us?*

FIRST WEEK OF ADVENT
HOPE CANDLE

Today, we light the first candle of Advent, the candle of Hope. This candle reminds us that even in the darkest of times, God's promises shine bright. Hope is not wishful thinking—it is the confident expectation that God is who He says He is and will do what He has promised.

As we wait for the coming of Christ, we hold fast to this hope. Just as the prophets of old longed for the Messiah, we, too, wait with anticipation for His presence to break into our lives. Hope steadies us when fear rises and provides us strength when we feel weak.

We wait in hope for the Lord; He is our help and our shield (Psalm 33:20). This first candle reminds us to lift our eyes toward God's faithfulness and to trust that His light will never be overcome by darkness.

PRAYER

Lord, as we light the candle of Hope, remind us that Your promises never fail. Even when the world feels dark or uncertain, You are our help and our shield. Plant Your hope deep within our hearts this Advent, and teach us to wait with trust and confidence in You. Amen.

SCRIPTURE VERSES TO READ & REFLECT

- Isaiah 11:1–2
- Micah 5:2
- Luke 1:30–33

OPENNESS

Sometimes, the only way to tackle a project is to know what the primary goal is. What's your 'why' (why are you doing this)? So, let's begin with your 'why' for Advent and Christmas, or rather, your reason for the season.

Can you relate to the answers below on why you do what you do?

- Because I have always done these things, it's tradition.
- If I don't, then Christmas won't happen.
- To draw me closer to the Lord.
- Honestly? I don't know why I even bother.

I have had all four responses at one point or another! When you know your 'why', you will keep from getting caught up in the chaos that comes with the holidays. As I mentioned in the introduction, if our focus is to draw closer to Jesus, then He will supply us with the 'why' for our Advent "project." How do we find that 'why?' By being open with God.

Take time out of your day to start a conversation with God. When you do this, not only give Him your concerns, but also praise, thanksgiving, and confess your sins. Once you have done this, take a moment to pause and wait for a response or clarity. The first step to becoming open with God is waiting for Him to respond to you. His answers can be both delightful and challenging, but being open means trusting in Him and His plans for you.

Openness is the soil where God plants His Spirit. Advent invites us to surrender our plans and receive Christ afresh.

When we approach Advent with openness, we begin to see that our 'why' isn't about checking off traditions or keeping up appearances. It becomes about preparing a place in our hearts where Christ can dwell. This means slowing down enough to notice His presence in the ordinary—lighting a candle, reading a verse, offering a prayer. These small acts, when done with intention, become sacred moments that align us with God's greater story. Advent reminds us that we don't need to strive to make Christmas "perfect." Instead, we are invited to welcome Perfection Himself—Jesus—into our imperfect lives.

> *Rejoice in the Lord always; again I will say, Rejoice. Let your gentleness be known to everyone. The Lord is near. Do not worry about anything, but in everything by prayer and supplication with thanksgiving let your requests be made known to God* (Philippians 4:4-6).

PRAYER

Lord, open my heart to Your Spirit. Make room in me for Your will this Advent.

TAKE TIME TO...

- Make a list of what you would like to happen during Advent as you prepare for the Christmas season. Remember when you make your list, ask yourself, 'Will doing these things bring me or others closer to God?'
- Remain open today and watch God work things out for good (Romans 8:28).

SCRIPTURE VERSES TO READ & REFLECT

- Luke 1:26–38
- Romans 8:28
- Psalm 139:23–24

JOURNAL PROMPT

What is your 'why' for this Advent? How can openness reshape it?

ANTICIPATION

We will begin today with Titus 2:13, *while we wait for the blessed hope and the manifestation of the glory of our great God and Savior, Jesus Christ.* This Scripture verse is often read at Midnight Mass to remind us of God's fulfilling promise of salvation in the person of Jesus Christ. The word Advent comes from the Latin word that means 'coming',[1] and to anticipate is defined as 'expecting something to take place.'[2] So when we anticipate Advent, we are essentially expecting something to come. The purpose of Advent is to prepare and wait expectantly for the coming of our Lord Jesus Christ.

Did you know that you are the reason God gave us His only Son? God loves you and has so much to offer you. It is about slowing down just enough to notice His presence and prepare your heart for Him. It is easy to become so caught up in the blur of festivities that we forget to slow down and take time from our day to be with Jesus. In the morning, you start off with prayer, and the next thing you know, it is 9 o'clock in the evening, and you are ready for bed.

Can you remember what it was like to look forward to something? Advent challenges us to look forward to and expect something to happen. When is the last time you expected something from God? Today, I give you permission to daydream and anticipate God revealing Himself to you this Advent and Christmas season.

Advent anticipation is holy longing. Like Israel, we wait expectantly for God to act in our lives. This holy longing is not a passive waiting but an active posture of the heart. Anticipation calls us to lean in with hope, to trust that God is at work even when we cannot see it. Just as a child eagerly counts down the days until Christmas morning, we, too, are invited to wait with wonder and expectation. Our anticipation becomes a declaration of faith—believing that the God who came before, and who is present now, will come again with promises fulfilled.

PRAYER

Lord, awaken holy expectation in me. Teach me to watch for Your presence.

TAKE TIME TO:

- Pacing yourself is a great way to see God at work in your life. Try to make a conscious effort to pause here and there throughout the day and ask yourself, 'Where have I seen the glory of God today?'
- In what ways are you anticipating God to reveal Himself? Then do as Jesus' mother Mary did by pondering on such things and holding them close to your heart.
- Before you go to sleep, reflect on these things and give God praise.

SCRIPTURE VERSES TO READ & REFLECT

- Psalm 62:6–9
- Proverbs 23:18
- Isaiah 40:31

JOURNAL PROMPT

What are you expecting God to do this week? Where will you watch for Him?

WAITING

Sometimes when waiting for something, you may be tempted to fill the void by finding something else to do. Have you ever had an extra five minutes and thought, 'Oh, I should get this done quick.' I know I have. What if we looked at these extra nuggets of time as opportunities to stop and pray or read Scripture? How would you feel about stopping for a minute to breathe and spend it with God? Would you feel stressed that you may not be able to get your entire to-do list accomplished for the day, or would you feel more at peace?

> *Now as they went on their way, he entered a certain village, where a woman named Martha welcomed him into her home. She had a sister named Mary, who sat at the Lord's feet and listened to what he was saying. But Martha was distracted by her many tasks; so she came to him and asked, "Lord, do you not care that my sister has left me to do all the work by myself? Tell her then to help me." But the Lord answered her, "Martha, Martha, you are worried and distracted by many things; there is need of only one thing. Mary has chosen the better part, which will not be taken away from her"* (Luke 10:38-42).

Lord, do you not care I am left by myself to do the _____? How would you fill in this blank? I could fill it in with a few things, such as Christmas Cards, making sure gifts get to family, friends, and neighbors, etc. As I begin thinking of more things to fill in the blank with, it makes me start to relate to Martha on a personal level. However, Mary gives us the example of how we are to take time to listen and wait upon the Lord. Remember, your 'why' this Advent is to go deeper with the Lord and to share Him with others. To do so, you must stop and sit at the Lord's feet to listen as He speaks.

Waiting with Jesus is not wasted time; it becomes the place where intimacy grows and priorities realign. Waiting teaches us to trust that God's timing is always better than our own. It stretches our faith and reminds us that we are not the ones in control—He is. When we surrender the urge to rush ahead, we discover that God often uses the waiting season to prepare our hearts for what is to come. The pause is not empty; it is purposeful. In the stillness, God refines us, strengthens us, and reminds us that His presence is the true gift we are longing for.

PRAYER

Jesus, help me choose the better part—sitting with You rather than rushing past You.

TAKE TIME TO...

- Today, your challenge will be to take a couple of minutes to stop and rest at the Lord's feet, either by rereading the Scripture verse above or the extra Scripture verse listed below. How do you feel when you are in Martha mode?
- After performing today's challenge, how did it feel to rest and wait on the Lord like Mary?

SCRIPTURE VERSES TO READ AND REFLECT

- Isaiah 30:18–21
- Psalm 27:13–14
- Lamentations 3:25–26

JOURNAL PROMPT

How do you typically respond to waiting—and how could you invite Jesus into it?

HOLINESS

Once we begin to get too busy, we can drift away from a state of peace. When we slow down, a state of peace immediately consumes us.

Ephesians 4:23-24 states, *and to be renewed in the spirit of your minds, and to clothe yourselves with the new self, created according to the likeness of God in true righteousness and holiness* (NASB). To be holy is to strive to be better than before. It is not on our own account that we obtain righteousness. God alone is the one who supplies us with the grace necessary to strive for holiness. We are made in the image and likeness of God, in which the precious blood of Jesus has redeemed us and has destined us to enjoy Heaven with Him for all eternity.

You are here because you want to grow intimate with God. Your heart and soul are restless and can get caught up and swept away in the chaos and noise if they are not kept in check. Now is the time to take hold of the things that take you away from intimacy with Jesus. Your pursuit of holiness will bring glory to God. And when you go deeper with God, you will be renewed and transformed.

There is a time and a season for you. Think of this Advent season as a time to reset your focus on what matters most. Earlier this week, we established our purpose to draw closer to God and to show the light of Christ to others. This is our reason to remain open as we wait and prepare our hearts with anticipation for the Nativity of our Lord Jesus Christ.

Holiness is not a distant, unreachable goal but a daily choice to live set apart for Christ. It is seen in the small things — in the way you speak, serve, forgive, and love. Each act of obedience, no matter how ordinary, shapes you into the likeness of Jesus. Advent reminds us that holiness is not about perfection but about walking with God moment by moment, allowing His Spirit to sanctify and strengthen us along the way.

Holiness is God's invitation to wholeness — daily surrender that renews the mind and reflects Christ. When we embrace this calling, we begin to see it as a gift rather than a burden. It is not about striving harder in our own strength, but about allowing the Spirit to transform us from within. A life rooted in prayer, worship, and quiet moments of surrender naturally reflects Jesus to the world around us. The more time we spend in His presence, the more His character becomes visible in our own. This season is an opportunity to make room in your heart where Christ can dwell freely, shaping your thoughts, words, and actions into a living testimony of His love.

PRAYER

Father, renew my mind and clothe me with Your holiness.

TAKE TIME TO...

- Take some time to rest and look at all the ways you were blessed this week.
- Ask God to help you as you attempt to change your mind towards an attitude of righteousness and holiness.

SCRIPTURE VERSES TO READ & REFLECT

- Psalm 8
- Hebrews 12:14
- 1 Peter 1:15–16

JOURNAL PROMPT

Which habit or thought needs renewal to pursue holiness this season?

WEEK TWO

PEACE

WEEKEND REFLECTION
PEACE

A REFLECTION ON THE ANNUNCIATION

The Annunciation is one of the most pivotal moments in all of salvation history. In Luke 1:26–38, the angel Gabriel announces God's plan, and Mary responds with her courageous *fiat*: *"Let it be done to me according to your word."* With that humble "yes," the Word became flesh. Mary's surrender opened the door for God's Divine plan of salvation to begin.

Mary's *yes* meant immense change, uncertainty, and sacrifice. Yet her obedience shows us the transformative power of trust. Unlike Adam's disobedience, which brought sin into the world, Mary's obedience ushered in life and salvation. Her faith reminds us that one act of surrender to God can change everything.

This passage also reveals the heart of the Incarnation: God Himself chose to dwell among us, to walk in our struggles, and to show us the way of love. At the perfect time and in the place He ordained, He sent His Son into the world, choosing Mary as the vessel of His Divine plan. This is not only history—it is the miracle of a God who loves us so deeply that nothing is impossible for Him.

Peace flows out of this mystery. True peace is not the absence of trials or suffering, but the presence of Christ with us in all things—our joys and our struggles. When we say,

"Peace be with you," we are really speaking the peace of Jesus Christ into one another's lives. It is reconciliation—letting go of resentments and forgiving from the heart. It is unity—reminding us that we are one body, bound together in His love.

Mary's example challenges us to embrace God's will with the same courage and openness. Saying *yes* to God may feel risky, but it brings us into His greater purpose and opens our hearts to His transforming grace. Her faith invites us to ask: Are we willing to surrender our plans, so God can work through us?

Obedience is not weakness but strength. It frees us from control and fear, allowing God's love to flow through us. Just as Mary's *yes* changed the course of history, our own *yes* to God can bring light and hope to the world around us.

The Annunciation is more than a story—it is a call. A call to faith. A call to courage. A call to surrender. Above all, it is a call to peace—the peace of Christ that accompanies us wherever He guides us.

PRAYER

Lord, just as Mary said yes to You, give me the courage to do the same. Help me to trust You even when the path is uncertain. May Your peace reign in my heart—not the absence of trials, but the presence of Your love in every moment. Teach me to forgive, to reconcile, and to live in unity with others. Here I am, Lord—let it be done to me according to Your word. Amen.

QUESTIONS FOR REFLECTION

1. How does Mary's "yes" inspire you in your own journey of faith?

2. Where in your life do you struggle to find peace, and how might inviting Christ into those places change your perspective?

3. Are there areas where God is asking you to surrender control and trust Him more fully?

SECOND WEEK OF ADVENT
PEACE CANDLE

The second purple candle is the Candle of Peace, often called the Bethlehem Candle. It reminds us of Mary and Joseph's journey to Bethlehem. Though their path was filled with uncertainty, God was faithful to guide them each step of the way.

This candle invites us to place our trust in Christ, our true source of peace. Today, we light the second candle of Advent, the candle of Peace. Jesus, our Prince of Peace, calms the storms in our lives and draws us back into the Father's love. *You will keep in perfect peace those whose minds are steadfast, because they trust in You* (Isaiah 26:3 NIV).

PRAYER

Lord Jesus, Prince of Peace, as we light this candle, calm the storms within our hearts and remind us that You are near. Just as You guided Mary and Joseph on their journey, guide us through our uncertainties with Your steady hand. Fill us with Your peace that passes all understanding, and help us to share that peace with those around us. Amen.

SCRIPTURE VERSES TO READ & REFLECT

- Isaiah 26:3–4
- Isaiah 9:6
- John 14:27

MERCY

Let's face it, the holidays can either be joyous or a difficult time when it comes to being with loved ones. As I thought about this, I reflected back to when our adult girls were young. They have always had a close relationship. There were days they played together, laughing and having fun, and then there were days they would fight. But at the end of the day, they would always make amends.

As families grow older, sometimes it becomes harder to make amends with one another. This can happen for several reasons, but whatever the reason, it is important we make amends with those around us; not only because it is the right thing to do, but because we never know how those strained relationships are affecting those closest to us as well. God wants us to love one another, and it is never His will for families to drift apart.

As we enter into the Advent season, we step into a season of mercy. God is the one who, despite all our shortcomings, offers His mercy to us repeatedly. Mercy is a gift of salvation. The time you are spending with Him is now preparing your heart to give the gift of mercy to others.

> *As God's chosen ones, holy and beloved, clothe yourselves with compassion, kindness, humility, meekness, and patience. Bear with one another and, if anyone has a complaint against another, forgive each other; just as the Lord has forgiven you, so you also must forgive* (Colossians 3:12-13 NASB).

We are told to extend compassion, kindness, humility, meekness, patience, and forgiveness. Sometimes this comes easily, while other times it feels like the hardest thing to give.

Whatever the situation may be, you can ask God to show you how. He has wrapped us in compassion, and through receiving His forgiveness, we learn to extend that same grace and mercy to others.

The gift of mercy has the power to soften hearts and heal what seems unfixable. It begins with a willingness to lay down pride and choose love over being "right." When we forgive, we mirror the heart of Christ, who gave freely even when we did not deserve it.

In this season, think of reconciliation as a bridge—connecting what has been broken and offering a way back to peace. It may take courage, and it may take time, but every step in that direction opens the door for God's grace to flow into your family and relationships.

PRAYER

Merciful God, help me to forgive as I have been forgiven.

TAKE TIME TO...

During your prayer time this week, ask God to place on your heart anyone He wants you to offer mercy to this Advent or Christmas season. Then anticipate Him to help you in a mighty way when the time comes.

SCRIPTURE VERSES TO READ & REFLECT

- Philippians 2:3–4
- Micah 6:8
- Ephesians 4:2

JOURNAL PROMPT

Who needs your mercy or a fresh start? What first step can you take?

BREATHE

I once heard, "Be careful what you pray for, especially when it comes to praying for more patience." Often, the answer to your prayer comes with plenty of opportunities to exercise such a request (if you catch my drift). When we have our plates full, it's easy to lose patience with others. This is why it was necessary to establish your "why."

Romans 12:12 reminds us, *Rejoice in hope, be patient in suffering, persevere in prayer* (NASB). Did you notice the last part of the verse says, *"to persevere in prayer?"* This is why you must give yourself a time-out during the day to pray. The holidays bring more people into your life than any other time of the year. The opportunities to bring Christ to others are limitless. The season of Advent presents a great opportunity to prepare our hearts for the Lord, so we will be ready to share Him with others.

Here is a little exercise to help you the next time you are about to lose your patience. Take a deep breath in, and then exhale slowly. However, when you do so, say to yourself, *"Breathe in Christ,"* and when you exhale, say to yourself, *"Breathe out (insert your name here)."* This simple exercise has saved me many times from saying something I would later regret.

Patience is not something we master once and for all—it is something God continually grows in us through daily choices. Each pause to breathe, each whispered prayer, and each decision to respond with kindness instead of frustration creates space for His Spirit to work in us. Advent reminds us that waiting itself can be holy when we allow the waiting to transform our hearts. In every delay, every long line, and every challenging moment, God is shaping us into people who reflect His peace.

We can't do this without Him. God shows us patience as we stumble and fall, only to repent and get back up and begin again. So prepare your heart and be ready to just breathe. In doing so, the light of Christ will shine so brightly.

In busy seasons, patience grows as we return to prayerful breathing—receiving Christ, releasing self. Breathing is more than a physical act—it is a spiritual reminder that God is as close as our very breath. Each inhale is a gift of life from Him, and each exhale is a release of the burdens we try to carry on our own. When we learn to pause and breathe with intention, we invite Christ to steady our hearts and quiet our minds. This Advent, let your breath become a prayer, a rhythm that keeps you centered on the One who gives true peace in the middle of the season's noise.

PRAYER

Prince of Peace, slow my pace and steady my breath in Your love.

TAKE TIME TO...

- The next time you feel your patience wearing thin, try the breathing exercise.
- Don't forget to be kind and patient with yourself.

SCRIPTURE VERSES TO READ & REFLECT

- Galatians 5:22–23
- 1 Corinthians 13:4–7
- Psalm 131:2

JOURNAL PROMPT

When patience thins, try the 'breathe in Christ, breathe out self' prayer. What changed?

KINDNESS

Today, I would like to talk about the gift of spreading a little kindness this season. The perfect example of this gift is found in John 3:16: *"For God so loved the world that he gave his only Son, so that everyone who believes in him may not perish but may have eternal life."*

This verse reminds us that true love puts others first. To live this out means thinking of ourselves less and others more. A simple gesture can change the heart and mind of a person, and the world we live in today could greatly benefit from such acts. Whether it is a smile, a kind word, or taking time to listen, these are all gifts that cost us little but mean so much.

Sometimes it is easy to take our loved ones for granted, and at the end of the day, our patience can run thin. Yet those closest to us deserve the same gentle spirit we so often extend to strangers. When I felt called to share the spirit of Christmas while shopping, I started by offering a smile to those I passed. As my confidence grew, I began to greet people or simply be mindful not to rush past them. I cannot say if anyone's day was changed, but I noticed that mine was. The saying, *"What you give to others comes back to you,"* rang true in those moments.

Simple actions—whether a smile, a gentle word, or patience in a busy moment—become like small candles lit in the darkness. They may seem ordinary, but God can use even the smallest spark to warm a weary heart. In this season of preparation, what better gift can we give than to reflect Christ's love through compassion, thoughtfulness, and care for those around us?

When we practice kindness, we are planting seeds that we may never see bloom. A simple act could be the encouragement someone needs to keep going, the reminder that they are not invisible, or the glimpse of God's love they have been longing for. You may never know the impact of a gentle word or small gesture, but Heaven sees—and God delights in using what appears small to bring about something far greater..

Kindness is love put into motion. It doesn't require grand gestures; often, it's the unnoticed acts—holding a door, offering encouragement, or listening—that leave the deepest impact. By slowing down and being attentive, we reflect the reality that Christ's love is here, present, and available to all.

PRAYER

Lord, make me an instrument of Your kindness today.

TAKE TIME TO...

- The next time you are around people, show kindness, whether it is with a hello, a smile, or a Christmas blessing of "Merry Christmas."
- Think of someone who would benefit from a random gift of kindness from you.

SCRIPTURE VERSES TO READ & REFLECT

- Ephesians 4:32
- Colossians 3:12
- Proverbs 11:17

JOURNAL PROMPT

Choose one tangible act of kindness you will do today. For whom?

RESTORATION

Today, I would like you to reflect on these past two weeks. Have you been able to slow down for Advent? What do you want Jesus to fulfill for you this Advent Season? It is never too late to ask Him.

One of my favorite things to do is to get up early in the morning before everyone is awake, make myself a strong cup of coffee, and spend time reading Scripture and praying. When I miss this quiet time with the Lord, I start to feel unsettled inside—a deep longing rises in me to be renewed and restored.

> *You who have made me see many troubles and calamities will revive me again; from the depths of the earth you will bring me up again. You will increase my honor, and comfort me once again* (Psalm 71:20-21 NASB).

God knows you and all you are doing for the Christmas season as you make way for Him. Don't let God be lost in your extra activities of writing notes in Christmas cards, buying and wrapping gifts, decorating your home, and celebrating with others. Instead, as you go about these activities, ask yourself, *"Where is God in this?"*—am I aware of His presence and reflecting His love through what I'm doing? You will have a different mind-set when you approach these extra activities in this way. The Scripture verse reminds us to slow down and rest, for God will revive and comfort you. He will restore you until your cup overflows.

When you slow down, it is like driving down a hill while using your brakes—you still get to where you need to be, but at a much safer pace.

Restoration is not just about catching your breath; it is about allowing God to reshape your heart in the process. When you invite Him into your moments of exhaustion or overextension, He gently reminds you that His strength is made perfect in weakness. Renewal begins when you shift from striving to abiding—letting His Spirit fill the empty places and restore your joy. Slowing down to notice His presence revives weary hearts and strengthens the soul.

This kind of renewal doesn't happen in a hurry—it unfolds when we create space for God to move. Advent is that sacred pause where we let go of the pressure to do it all and remember that Christ has already done it all for us. In His presence, our restless hearts find rest, our burdens are lifted, and our souls are refreshed. God's invitation is to trade weariness for His peace, striving for His grace, and busyness for His abiding love.

PRAYER

God, restore my soul and revive my hope in You.

TAKE TIME TO...

- Reflect on the fruits you have received from slowing down and spending it with the Lord. What have the benefits been in doing so?
- Give God thanks and praise.

SCRIPTURE VERSES TO READ & REFLECT

- Psalm 46:10
- Isaiah 40:29–31
- Matthew 11:28–30

JOURNAL PROMPT

Where do you need God's restoration? Name it and ask Him to restore you.

_____

_____

_____

_____

_____

_____

_____

_____

_____

_____

_____

_____

_____

_____

_____

_____

_____

WEEK THREE

JOY

WEEKEND REFLECTION
JOY

JOURNEY TO BETHLEHEM

Joy is more than happiness or fleeting emotions. Happiness often depends on circumstances, but joy is something much deeper — it is a gift of the Holy Spirit. This kind of joy is rooted in trusting God and His perfect plan, even when life doesn't make sense. It's the quiet strength that steadies us, the peace that carries us through trials, and the contentment that reminds us God is always with us.

When I talk about joy, I don't mean pretending everything is fine. True joy comes when we lean into God's love, when we choose to believe His promises in the middle of our struggles. It's a choice — a choice to love Him, to trust Him, and to let His Spirit fill us. Joy isn't automatic; it grows as we stay close to Jesus and allow Him to shape our hearts.

This week, we journey with Mary and Joseph toward Bethlehem (Matthew 1:18–24; Luke 2:1–5). Their path was difficult, yet it was filled with anticipation and joy — for God's promise was being fulfilled.

The third Sunday of Advent is Gaudete Sunday, "Rejoice!" Joy is more than happiness; it is rooted in God's presence. Happiness fades when circumstances change, but joy is steady because it comes from Christ.

In my life, joy often sneaks in unexpectedly — a conversation with a friend, laughter with family, or seeing God answer a prayer in ways I didn't expect. Joy reminds me that even in hardships, God's goodness still breaks through. Advent joy calls us to lift our heads and rejoice that the Lord has come, is coming, and will come again.

This kind of joy also spills over into the way we live. When we choose joy, we shine God's love in a way that others can see. A joyful spirit becomes a testimony, drawing others to the hope we have in Christ. Think of it as a light in the darkness — joy points people back to Jesus, the true source of life.

Joy is not found in the busyness of the season or in our accomplishments, but in Christ Himself. He is the One who satisfies us, who gives us peace that lasts, and who teaches us to love others well. By living in that joy, we strengthen our faith, build deeper connections with others, and inspire those around us to seek the same gift.

So let us choose joy — not the kind that fades when life gets hard, but the joy that is anchored in God's unchanging presence. This joy empowers us to face challenges with courage, steadies our hearts with hope, and transforms even the most ordinary moments into opportunities for grace.

PRAYER

Lord Jesus, You are my joy and my strength. In a world that often weighs me down with worries and distractions, remind me that true joy is found only in You. Teach me to rejoice not because everything is perfect, but because You are present with me in every moment. Like Mary and Joseph, help me to walk faithfully on the journey, trusting that Your promises are being fulfilled. Fill my heart with laughter, peace, and gratitude, and let my life reflect Your goodness so that others may be drawn to the joy that only You can give. Amen.

QUESTIONS FOR REFLECTION

1. What brings you joy this Advent season?

2. How does joy differ from happiness in your life?

3. How can you share joy with someone who feels weary or burdened?

THIRD WEEK OF ADVENT
JOY CANDLE

The third candle is pink and is known as the "Shepherd's Candle." It represents the joy of the shepherds when the angels announced the birth of Jesus, and the joy of God's people as we arrive at the halfway point of Advent. The rose color breaking into the violet reminds us that our waiting is nearly complete. Today, we light the candle of joy. True joy is not found in our circumstances but in the presence of God with us. *The joy of the Lord is my strength* (Nehemiah 8:10).

PRAYER

Lord Jesus, You are my joy and my strength. As we light the candle of joy, remind us that true joy is not found in what happens around us, but in Your presence with us. Fill our hearts with gladness, and help us to share that joy with others this Advent. Amen.

SCRIPTURE VERSES TO READ & REFLECT

- Matthew 1:18–24
- Luke 2:1–5
- Nehemiah 8:9–10

FAITH

To experience a simple Advent is to have faith that all will work out for the good. Do you have this type of faith? I'm not there yet, but I am further along than I used to be. What does it take to have an extraordinary faith?

Let's look at Romans 1:5, *through whom we have received grace and apostleship to bring about the obedience of faith among all the Gentiles for the sake of his name* (NASB).

Faith is more than a thought or feeling; it is a response. To be obedient to God's Will reveals the size of our faith in Him. Faith begins with the act of trusting in God, but becomes extraordinary when we are obedient to His Will and give our entire selves to Him. The result of a person's faith is revealed through the outpouring of charity, and as our faith in God increases, the outpouring of our love increases as well.

Here are three ways to increase your faith:

1. Read the Bible
2. Reflect on the Word
3. Live out the Word of God with love

When you read Scriptures, you will know God more; they are love letters written by Him for you. The more you come to know Him, the deeper your desire will be to follow and obey Him. How do we be obedient to God? By listening to His call for us and by following the Commandments. When you trust God and say *yes* your faith will grow, and others will see it.

Faith matures through obedience. As we take in God's Word and open our hearts to listen, our response becomes an outpouring of love—love that cannot help but overflow to those around us. Trust grows strongest when it is tested. It is in the seasons of uncertainty, when answers are delayed or the path feels unclear, that we learn to lean fully on God. Waiting is never wasted when it is offered to Him. Each time you choose to believe His promises over your fears, you are declaring that He is faithful and worthy of your surrender. Living with trust doesn't mean having all the answers—it means resting in the truth that God already does.

PRAYER

Lord, increase my faith and make me obedient to Your Word.

TAKE TIME TO...

- Write down one thing you desire in your life and begin to expect a real change to occur.
- Then try the faith exercise listed above.

SCRIPTURE VERSE TO READ & REFLECT

- Hebrews 11:1–6
- James 2:14–18
- Psalm 37:3–6

JOURNAL PROMPT

What step of obedience is God asking of you?

HOPE

The definition of hope is 'a feeling of expectation or desire for a certain thing to happen.' Hope responds to the aspiration of happiness which God has placed in the heart of every woman and man, and inspires a person's activities and purifies them for the kingdom of Heaven. Hope keeps a man from discouragement, sustains a person during times of abandonment, and opens up their heart in expectation of eternal beatitude. Buoyed up by hope, the person is preserved from selfishness and led to the happiness that flows from charity.

Satan wants us to be hopeless because when we are hopeless, we begin to lose our faith. Have you ever experienced a time in your life when despair had set in? I have seen it in people whom I love dearly, and I am here to say it is such a helpless feeling to watch. It is as if they cannot see around the corner, the good God is working out for them. They become negative and begin to doubt everything and everyone. You can almost see life draining from their demeanor.

Oftentimes what is at the root of hopelessness is a distant relationship with God. The best way to get back on track is to read Scripture. The Psalms are my favorite because David had obstacles in his life that looked hopeless, but instead of throwing the towel in, he went to God and poured out his despair.

Romans 15:13, *May the God of hope fill you with all joy and peace in believing, so that by the power of the Holy Spirit you may abound in hope* (NASB). It is easy to have hope when everything is good, but it is in times of suffering and discouragement that hope is not so easy to hold onto. We are most awakened when we draw our attention to the emotional memory of God who became a child. When you think about your memories from youth until now, can you remember the first time you recognized the meaning of Christmas? What can you remember? As Romans 15:13 states, God fills us with joy and peace through the power of the Holy Spirit. Hope gives you joy and peace.

Hope anchors the soul in God's promises, especially in discouraging times. It is more than wishful thinking—it is the confident assurance that God is who He says He is and will do what He has promised. This season calls us to cling to His truth, even when circumstances feel heavy or uncertain. Just as the prophets held fast to the promise of a coming Messiah, we too are invited to trust God's Word in our own lives. Every candle lit on the wreath reminds us that even the smallest light can pierce the deepest darkness, and that Christ, our ultimate assurance, has already come and will come again.

PRAYER

God of hope, fill me with joy and peace in believing.

TAKE TIME TO...

- Today, take time to reflect on the first time you realized the meaning of Christmas. Can you remember? How old were you?

SCRIPTURE VERSES TO READ & REFLECT

- 1 Timothy 6:17
- Psalm 42:11
- Romans 5:3–5

JOURNAL PROMPT

Where are you tempted to lose hope? What promise will you cling to?

LOVE

The best example of love is demonstrated by the Nativity of the Lord. God the Father demonstrated His love for us when He took on flesh to dwell with man; the living God became visible to all. The love God demonstrated is called Agape love, and is the highest form of love - sacrificial love. In other words, Agape love is the kind of love you demonstrate when you put others and their needs above your own.[3]

God's love was revealed among us in this way: God sent his only Son into the world so that we might live through him. In this is love, not that we loved God but that he loved us and sent his Son to be the atoning sacrifice for our sins. Beloved, since God loved us so much, we also ought to love one another (1 John 4:9-11 CST). Dear friends, since God so loved us, we also ought to love one another. We are sinners, and yet God wanted us to be with Him. God offered us mercy by giving up His only Son so we, too, could be with Him one day. This is agape love.

The last part of 1 John asks us to offer mercy to others as He has done for us. Remember, the definition of Agape love is to put others' needs above our own. Is there someone God is calling you to offer the gift of mercy and love to this Christmas season? What would this look like? Sometimes something as simple as a smile, a friendly greeting, or a kind note is all someone needs to completely turn around their day. God is in those simple gestures, and wants us to share Him with others - even through simple means.

We are called to do everything with the intention of love. This isn't always easy, especially as we prepare for the extra activities that come with Christmas, because we become overextended and tired. It is at these moments, when loving others can be a challenge, that we need to show love the most. It is important that as your activities increase, so should your time with Jesus and Scripture.

At the manger, we see agape—sacrificial devotion that calls us to care for others as we have been cared for. This is the mark of a heart transformed by Christ. When His presence fills us, it naturally shapes how we treat those around us—both the ones who are easy to embrace and the ones who stretch our patience. Now is the perfect time to ask God to expand your capacity to serve beyond your comfort zone. Each act of compassion, no matter how small, reflects the heart of Jesus who came not to be served but to serve. This Christmas season, let selfless love be the motivation behind every word, every action, and every gift you give.

PRAYER

Jesus, teach me to love as You love—sacrificially and sincerely.

TAKE TIME TO...

- What sets you off when you become overextended?
- Know your weaknesses and ask God to show you how to love unconditionally, especially during times of exhaustion.
- Remember, it is okay to give yourself a time-out when you become overwhelmed. Just breathe, pray, and ask God for help.

SCRIPTURE VERSES TO READ & REFLECT

- 1 Corinthians 13:1–7,13
- Romans 5:8
- John 15:12–13

JOURNAL PROMPT

Who is God calling you to love sacrificially this week?

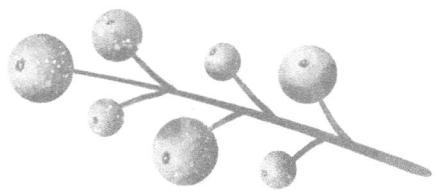

JOY

The third week of Advent invites us into a spirit of joy. Traditionally called Gaudete Week, it's a reminder to pause amid our waiting and recognize the nearness of Christ. Even in the midst of life's challenges, we are called to rejoice—not because everything is perfect, but because God is faithful and His promises are being fulfilled.

This season is an opportunity to reflect and look forward to celebrating Christmas with our loved ones. What reasons do we have to rejoice?

- The hope of healing that comes at Christmas.
- Remembering the birth of Jesus on that first holy night.
- Knowing the Savior was born to free us from sin.
- Anticipating His return when we will dwell with God, the angels, and the saints for all eternity.

The Lord is my strength and my shield; in him my heart trusts; so I am helped, and my heart exults (Psalm 28:7). Happiness can be fleeting, but the gladness of the Gospel is a choice. God supplies the strength to carry this gladness, and the way we live becomes a reflection of His presence. So, as you put together your Christmas cards, are you simply checking off a task, or are you spreading the light of Christ? Ask yourself this with each tradition, and you may discover where God is inviting you to slow down and draw nearer to Him. The world is searching for a Savior, and as you are filled with His love, you are ready to pour that love into the lives of others.

Joy is discovered when we notice Christ's presence in both the simple and the significant moments of life. It isn't tied to everything going perfectly, but to the assurance that God is near and working for our good. Choosing joy is an act of faith—it declares that His light is brighter than any shadow and His peace steadier than any storm. Let your joy be a quiet testimony that invites others to see Jesus shining through you.

Rejoicing also shifts our perspective. Instead of focusing on what is missing or what has gone wrong, we begin to see the blessings God has already placed in our lives. Gratitude fuels gladness, and gladness strengthens faith. When you pause to thank God for even the smallest gifts—a kind word, a quiet moment, a reminder of His faithfulness—you cultivate a heart that rejoices naturally. This posture not only lifts your spirit but also becomes a witness to others that true joy is found in Christ alone.

PRAYER

Lord, restore to me the joy of Your salvation.

TAKE TIME TO...

- What ways have you felt God's joy this Advent? Write them down and give Him praise.
- In this busy time, try to make time to have coffee or a meal with your friends and loved ones to share the joy of the upcoming celebration of Christmas.

SCRIPTURE VERSES TO READ & REFLECT

- Nehemiah 8:10
- Psalm 16:11
- John 15:11

JOURNAL PROMPT

List three places you noticed God's joy recently.

WEEK FOUR

LOVE

WEEKEND REFLECTION
LOVE

THE BIRTH OF JESUS

The story of Jesus' birth is not a fable nor a legend but a real, historical event. St. Luke carefully records details that tie the birth of Christ to specific rulers, times, and places. Caesar Augustus, Quirinius, and Herod are all real historical figures. These details remind us that God entered into the reality of human history. Our faith is not built on myth, but on fact.

Jesus Christ truly was born in Bethlehem, truly lived among us, and truly entered into our humanity. He grew tired, felt hunger, and experienced joy, laughter, and sorrow—yet without sin. This is the beauty of the incarnation: God so loved the world that He came down, clothed in flesh, to dwell with us (John 1:14).

The angels announced to the shepherds—ordinary, humble workers—that a Savior had been born. Their fear turned into joy, and their night into light. God's message of salvation was not given first to kings and rulers but to the lowly, so that all may know: this gift is for everyone.

As we pause this weekend, let us remember that the manger points us to the cross. Jesus came not only to live among us but also to give His life for us. The tiny child wrapped in swaddling clothes would one day be wrapped in grave clothes and yet rise again so that we might share eternal life with Him.

So today, let us treasure this truth: *For God so loved the world that He gave His one and only Son, that whoever believes in Him shall not perish but have eternal life* (John 3:16).

Like Mary, let us ponder these things in our hearts. Like the shepherds, let us glorify and praise God for all that we have seen and heard. And like the angels, let us share the Good News of great joy—Christ the Lord has come! At Bethlehem, we behold Love made flesh. When our strength runs out, Christ's love flows where ours fails. We love because He first loved us.

PRAYER

Lord God, we thank You for sending Your Son into the world—not as a mighty king in a palace, but as a humble child born in a manger. Help us to pause and treasure the miracle of the incarnation. Fill us with the same joy the angels declared and the same wonder the shepherds felt. May we carry Your peace into our homes, our communities, and our world. Teach us to glorify and praise You in both small and great ways, and may the truth of Your love transform our hearts this Christmas and always. In Jesus' holy name, Amen.

QUESTIONS FOR REFLECTION

1. How have you experienced God's love this Advent?

2. Who is God calling you to love tangibly this week?

3. How will you carry His love into Christmas Day?

FOURTH WEEK OF ADVENT
LOVE CANDLE

The last purple candle, the "Angel's Candle," stands for love and reminds us of the angels' message of peace on earth. We are lighting the fourth candle of Advent today, the Love candle. Sending His Son into the world shows how much God loves us. This candle reminds us that love is a gift we give, not just a gift we receive. God's love is sacrificial, unconditional, and endless, and as His children, we are invited to reflect that same love to others in both simple and profound ways.

PRAYER

Heavenly Father, as we light the candle of Love, we thank You for the gift of Your Son, Jesus, the greatest expression of love the world has ever known. Teach us to love as You love—sacrificially, unconditionally, and with open hearts. Fill us with compassion for those around us, and let Your love shine through us so others may see Christ in our lives. Amen.

SCRIPTURE VERSES TO READ & REFLECT

- Luke 2:1–20
- John 3:16
- 1 John 4:9–11
- 1 Corinthians 13:1–7, 13

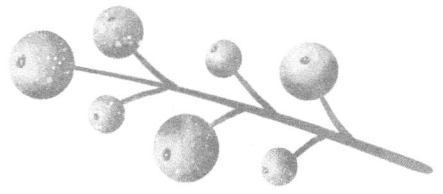

ORDINARY

When my husband, Pat, and I were first married, we were excited to celebrate our first Christmas together and talked about the different traditions we had with our families and what traditions we wanted to have in our new little family. Some of those traditions we've kept, others have faded away over time, and some we've added along the way. Traditions are good and a fun part of the holiday season, unless they drive you crazy and fill the season with chaos. Sometimes we run ourselves ragged as we try to make it all come together, and when it doesn't turn out the way we think it should, we discover ourselves feeling let down and disappointed.

I have gone through many Christmases of not being able to bring everything together like I had the year before, but in spite of this, everyone still has a great time. And I learned that the wonderful time didn't come from flashes of light and fanfare, but because of the small, ordinary things we did together. All it took to have the ideal Christmas was to worship, and for the family to be together, relax, laugh, and create memories.

When I contemplate the ordinary, I think about how the Messiah entered the world. There was no fancy hospital for Him; it was a cold and dark night, with no extra fuss. It made me wonder, 'If our savior was able to come into the world in such a simple way, why do I put all of this pressure on myself?' So I began to rethink traditions and all of my insane expectations and realized the best way to prepare is to make Advent a time to get my heart and mind right with what is most important. One day, while I was praying, I thought about whether I would let Jesus in if He knocked on my door on Christmas Eve, or if I would be too busy trying to make everything perfect. My first thought was, "Oh, I wish I had done this and that before You came, Lord." Then I remembered—Jesus entered the world in a humble stable, laid in a manger, surrounded by the animals that were kept there. The only thing really necessary for us to welcome Jesus is a ready heart.

While our family maintains various traditions, one thing remains constant: we love each other and we love Jesus. So keep it simple as we finish this Advent season and approach the day of our Lord's birth.

Always remember God delights to meet us in the ordinary; the humble stable reminds us to reset our expectations. The beauty of the ordinary is that it draws us back to what truly matters—presence over perfection. Sometimes the most meaningful moments happen when nothing is planned: a shared laugh around the table, a quiet prayer before bed, or a hug that lingers a little longer. These are the moments where God enters unnoticed, yet leaves the most profound impact. When we embrace simplicity, we find freedom from pressure and space for peace, the very gifts Christ chose to bring.

PRAYER

Immanuel, meet me in the ordinary and make my heart Your home.

TAKE TIME TO...

- Visit with your family and friends and ask them about their favorite memories from Christmas' past.
- Do one of your favorite ordinary activities today.

SCRIPTURE VERSES TO READ & REFLECT

- Luke 2:8–14
- Philippians 2:5–8
- Micah 5:2

JOURNAL PROMPT

Which pressure or tradition can you simplify to welcome Jesus?

REST

One of my favorite sayings is 'you cannot give what you don't have.' Oftentimes, when I have a long list of things to do, I will stay up late at night, only to find I can hardly function the next day; so much for getting things crossed off the to-do list. When you go nonstop, eventually something has to give, whether it is physically or spiritually. Advent is a perfect reminder to pace ourselves and give ourselves a time-out.

When I was growing up on the farm, there was always something for us to do, but every afternoon my grandpa would come in from chores and have a coffee break. No matter what everyone had on their chore list for the day, they would always stop what they were doing to gather together and rest, because they knew the importance of taking a break and spending time together throughout the day.

The best kind of break is one that refreshes the body, mind, and soul. If you were to ask me how to do this, I would recommend grabbing a cup of coffee (or tea if that is your fancy), a healthy snack, your devotional or Bible, and sitting down on your favorite couch or chair. Even just taking ten minutes to sip your coffee and read God's word is enough to leave you feeling rested and replenished. I know the temptation will be to keep on working through your lists and then take a break when you are finished, but as you've probably figured out, your to-do list is never truly finished. By setting a certain time in your day to take a break from your list, you will find that you are in a much better place, both physically and spiritually.

To have a simply Advent, why not take a break in your day to pause, rest, and reflect on how the Lord has provided for you thus far? It is time to take charge of your tasks and stop letting your tasks take charge of you.

Each week we have an opportunity to rest on the Sabbath. It allows us to pause and re-center our body and soul. Christ invites us to rest in Him even amid tasks. Rest is an act of trust. When we stop striving and step away from the endless demands, we are acknowledging that God is in control and that His strength is enough to carry what we cannot. Taking time to pause is not wasted—it is a declaration of faith that reminds us our worth is not measured by productivity but by being God's beloved. In those quiet pauses, we are renewed, not only for our own well-being, but also so that we can pour into others from a place of fullness rather than depletion.

PRAYER

Shepherd of my soul, lead me into true rest with You.

TAKE TIME TO...

- Set an alarm to remind you to stop, rest, and refuel.
- Have your Bible handy as well as a notebook. You never know, there may be something that will come to your mind to do for Him, or a special love note to encourage you.

SCRIPTURE VERSES TO READ & REFLECT

- Psalm 23:1–3
- Matthew 11:28–30
- Isaiah 30:15

JOURNAL PROMPT

Schedule a brief 'Sabbath pause' today. What difference did it make?

EXPECTATION

Have you ever been disappointed? When I was young, I would get caught up in the excitement and nostalgia of Christmas, only to experience disappointment upon its arrival. As I got older, I realized it was because my heart was not prepared for the real meaning of Christmas. I began to realize Christmas is more than a feeling; it is an expectation of something bigger. What is that something bigger? Jesus is the Messiah!

Sometimes, when you've had a series of disappointments, you may tell yourself to not get your hopes up. However, God wants you to have faith that He can bring the good into your life even in unexpected ways. Do you have the eyes to see the unexpected? If you don't expect anything good to happen, how will you notice it when it does? My hope at the start of Advent was to provide simple ways for you to spend more time with our Lord. Why? So you may expect to see God at work and all He has done for you. Christmas is a perfect reminder of how He sent His Son, Jesus, into the world for our salvation.

It is essential to have faith in the Lord and in His promises. God is longing for us to expect Him in all things, but we cannot do that unless we have faith in Him. We need to have faith that he will follow through for us and faith that He wants the good for our lives.

Are you asking God to touch your life and circumstances but not really expecting to see Him move at all? Our faith is what moves God. When you pray, you may ask God to act, yet doubt He truly will. Faith, however, is a deliberate choice—a decision of the will to trust Him even before you see the outcome. You can choose to believe that He will do great things for you, or you can choose to not believe; He will only move if you allow Him. Lift your expectations to God. Faith looks for His goodness and refuses cynicism.

Living with expectation means we lean forward into God's promises with a hopeful heart, even when the outcome is still unseen. It shifts our focus from what we lack to what He is preparing. Expectation doesn't guarantee everything will unfold the way we imagine, but it assures us that God's plan is always greater than ours. When we choose to expect His goodness, we begin to notice His fingerprints in the details of our lives—reminders that He is near, He is faithful, and He is working all things together for His glory and our good.

PRAYER

Faithful God, raise my expectations to match Your promises.

TAKE TIME TO...

- When is the last time you expected something good or big to happen? Do you recall what it was? Write it down in a journal.
- Read the additional Scripture verse to pray over your lack of faith.

SCRIPTURE VERSES TO READ & REFLECT

- Romans 8:24–25
- Psalm 27:13–14
- Hebrews 10:23

JOURNAL PROMPT

Write a prayer of expectation—what are you asking God to do?

REJOICE

The fourth week of Advent centers on the incredible love of the Father. It's the love that moved Him to send His Son into the world—not out of obligation, but out of deep, enduring compassion for us. This final week reminds us that the birth of Jesus is the ultimate expression of God's heart—a love willing to give everything so we might share in eternal life.

Do you recall the first week when I asked the question, "What do you want God to fulfill for you this Advent?" Did you ask Him? How did He reveal Himself to you?

This year, I asked God to "wow my socks off with His presence." One way I experienced this the most was with Christmas coffees. Normally, my family and I would host a Christmas party and invite neighbors and friends over, but this year I felt called to host coffees with friends, and what a gift I received during these times. I hosted eight Christmas coffees in five days and met with a total of twelve girlfriends. The time with my friends comprised laughter, celebrating a birthday, comforting a friend who had a family member pass away, and time with college friends that I had not seen in twenty years. God showed up in a big way, and His presence was overwhelming, leaving me in awe. He poured His love into me, and in return, I poured it out to others.

Your heart may have been empty at the beginning of Advent, but by spending time with the Lord, His love and presence have refueled it. God is searching for a home, a home in your heart. Advent prepared the way for Him, and Christmas is the opportunity for you to say, "Yes, Lord, I have room for you."

I would like to close our time with a prayer of blessing: *"May God be gracious to us and bless us and make his face to shine upon us, that your way may be known upon earth, your saving power among all nations. Let the peoples praise you, O God; let all the peoples praise you. Let the nations be glad and sing for joy, for you judge the peoples with equity and guide the nations upon earth. Let the peoples praise you, O God; let all the peoples praise you. The earth has yielded its increase; God, our God, has blessed us. May God continue to bless us; let all the ends of the earth revere Him." Amen* (Psalm 67).

Rejoicing is not just an expression of happiness—it is a posture of the heart that recognizes God's faithfulness in every season. When we take time to look back, we can see how He has carried us, how He has answered prayers in unexpected ways, and how His presence has never left us. This awareness naturally wells up in praise, not because life is perfect, but because His love is constant. To rejoice is to declare with confidence that God has come near and that His promises are true yesterday, today, and forever.

Thank you for joining me this Advent. Rejoice, because Love has shown us his Son, Emmanuel! Have a Merry Christmas!

PRAYER

Father, fill me with Your love that I may rejoice and bless others.

SCRIPTURE VERSES TO READ & REFLECT

- Psalm 67
- Philippians 4:4
- Luke 2:10–11

JOURNAL PROMPT

Take a few quiet moments to reflect on this season. Write down one way you have experienced God's love in a fresh way, one prayer He has answered (big or small), and one reason your heart is rejoicing as you enter into Christmas.

WELCOMING CHRIST

Advent has carried us through hope, peace, joy, and love. Each week, each reflection, and each Scripture has prepared our hearts to receive the greatest gift—Jesus Christ, Emmanuel, God with us. The waiting is over; the promise has been fulfilled.

Christmas reminds us that God came not in splendor but in simplicity. He entered our world as a child to dwell among us, to save us, and to show us the depth of His love. The manger teaches us that God delights to meet us in ordinary places, and that our hearts, however imperfect, can be His dwelling place when we welcome Him with openness.

As you step from Advent into the season of Christmas, carry with you the light of Christ. Let hope anchor you, let peace steady you, let joy strengthen you, and let love guide you. Remember that Advent was not just a season of preparation but the beginning of a lifelong invitation—to live each day with expectant hearts, watching for Emmanuel in the midst of ordinary life.

May the blessing of the newborn King rest upon you, may His light shine through you, and may His presence fill your days with everlasting joy. Rejoice, for Christ is born!

ENDNOTES

1. Advent. (2025). In Merriam-Webster Dictionary. https://www.merriam-webster.com/dictionary/Advent

2. anticipate. (2025). In Merriam-Webster Dictionary. https://www.merriam-webster.com/dictionary/anticipate

3. Lozano, A., & Lozano, A. (2025, June 16). Agape Love - Catholic Insight. Catholic Insight - Inspired by Truth, Enlightening Minds. https://catholicinsight.com/2020/01/16/agape-love/

ABOUT AUTHOR

Lisa Fahey is an author and speaker with over twenty years of experience working with youth, adults, and women in the church. She is the author of *Rise Up, Women of God: A Scripture Study on 1 John and 2 John*; *Simply: A Women's Study on Ecclesiastes*; *Simply Lent: A Journey of Reflection And Renewal With Jesus*; *Just As You Are: How Your Testimony Can Impact People In Ways You Never Thought Possible*; and *Restored: From Ordinary to Extraordinary*.

All are meant to inspire, encourage, and empower readers in their journey with God. Lisa draws on real-life stories and moments with God to inspire and encourage others.

At the age of 21, Lisa lost her first husband, which forever changed her approach to God and His Word. Through her work, she shares how God helped her to grow and rise up as a woman of God, even during the trials of life.

Although "life is hard and messy," Lisa can show her readers through her Bible studies and books that the key to experiencing life completely is to follow their calling by serving God.

If this book has blessed you, please share the message with others by posting on social media using #simplyadvent

Website
www.lisafahey.com

Podcast
Lisa Fahey Ministry (Apple & Spotify)

Follow Your Call Coaching
www.lisafahey.com/follow-your-call-coaching

Facebook
Christian Professional Women On Purpose - Lisa Fahey

Instagram
lisafaheyministry

Publishing
farmhousepublishings@gmail.com

OTHER TITLES BY LISA FAHEY

SIMPLY: A WOMEN'S BIBLE STUDY ON ECCLESIASTES

A six week study of Ecclesiastes. This book of wisdom teaches us that living simply is the secret to experiencing life to the fullest.

RISE UP, WOMEN OF GOD: A STUDY OF 1 JOHN & 2 JOHN

This six week study of 1 and 2 John are the ideal Epistles to guide us through life's questions and confusing times.

SIMPLY LENT: A JOURNEY OF REFLECTION AND RENEWAL WITH JESUS

Find calm, clarity, and Christ this Lent.

JUST AS YOU ARE: HOW YOUR TESTIMONY CAN IMPACT PEOPLE IN WAYS YOU NEVER THOUGHT POSSIBLE

Your testimony can reach people for Christ in ways you never thought possible.

RESTORED: FROM ORDINARY TO EXTRAORDINARY

Becoming the person God intended you to be… Extraordinary

www.ingramcontent.com/pod-product-compliance
Lightning Source LLC
Chambersburg PA
CBHW080225140626
46555CB00020B/3013

* 9 7 9 8 9 9 9 3 6 0 5 7 3 9 *